ANNA AKHMATOVA
Poems

Anna Akhmatova

POEMS

Selected and Translated by
LYN COFFIN

Introduction by Joseph Brodsky

W • W • NORTON & COMPANY
New York   London

The texts listed below were used in preparing these translations:

Anna Akhmatova, *Selected Works*. Moscow, 1974.
Anna Akhmoatova, *Works* (2 volumes). Munich: Inter-Language Literary Associates, 1965.

Some of these poems appeared previously in the *Michigan Quarterly Review*.

> *My special thanks to Serge Shishkoff,*
> *the sine qua non of this book,*
> *and much else*

Printed in the United States of America.

The text of this book is composed in Palatino, with
display type set in Melior. Composition and
manufacturing by The Maple-Vail Book Manufacturing Group.
Book design by A. Christopher Simon.

LIBRARY OF CONGRESS CATALOGING IN PUBLICATION DATA

Akhmatova, Anna Andreevna, 1889–1966.
  Poems.

  I. Coffin, Lyn., tr. II. Title.
PG3476.A324A23   1983   891.71'42   82–12502

ISBN 0-393-01567-X

ISBN 0-393-30014-5 (pbk.)

W. W. Norton & Company, Inc., 500 Fifth Avenue, New York, NY 10110
W. W. Norton & Company Ltd., 10 Coptic Street, London WC1A 1PU

2 3 4 5 6 7 8 9 0

In memory of
LAURA SUSAN RAMSAY

May 1957–May 1981
a ray of sunshine

CONTENTS

INTRODUCTION

When her father learned that his daughter was about to publish a selection of her poems in a St. Petersburg magazine, he called her in and told her that although he had nothing against her writing poetry, he'd urge her "not to befoul the good respected name" and to use a pseudonym. The daughter agreed, and this is how "Anna Akhmatova" entered Russian literature instead of Anna Gorenko.

The reason for this acquiescence was neither uncertainty about the elected occupation and her actual gifts nor anticipation of the benefits that a split identity can provide for a writer. It was done simply for the sake of "maintaining appearances" because among families belonging to the nobility—and Gorenko was one—the literary profession was generally regarded as somewhat unseemly and befitting those of more humble origins who didn't have a better way of making a name.

Still, the father's request was a bit of an overstatement. After all, the Gorenkos weren't princes. But then again the family lived in Tsarskoe Selo—Tsar's Village—which was the summer residence of the Imperial family, and this sort of topography could have influenced the man. For his seventeen-year-old daughter, however, the place had a different significance: Tzarskoye was the seat of the Lyceum in whose gardens a century ago "carelessly blossomed" young Pushkin.

As for the pseudonym itself, its choice had to do with the maternal ancestry of Anna Gorenko, which could be traced back to the last khan of the Golden Horde: to Achmat-khan, descendant of Chengiz-khan. "I am a Chengizite," she used to remark not without a touch of pride; and for a Russian ear "Akhmatova" has a distinct Oriental, Tartar to be precise, flavor. She didn't mean to be exotic, though, if only because in Russia a name with a Tartar overtone meets not curiosity but prejudice.

All the same, the five open *a*'s of Anna Akhmatova had a hypnotic effect and put this name's carrier firmly on top of the alphabet of Russian poetry. In a sense, it was her first successful line; memorable in its acoustic inevitability, with its *Ah* sponsored less by sentiment than by history. This tells you a lot about the intuition and quality of the ear of this seventeen-year-old girl who soon after publication began to sign her letters and legal papers as Anna Akhmatova. In its suggestion of identity derived from the fusion of sound and time, the choice of the pseudonym turned out to be prophetic.

Anna Akhmatova belongs to the category of poets who have neither genealogy nor discernible "development." She is the kind of poet that simply "happens";

that arrives into the world with an already established diction and his/her own unique sensibility. She came fully equipped, and she never resembled anyone. What was perhaps more significant is that none of her countless imitators was ever capable of producing a convincing Akhmatova pastiche either; they'd end up resembling one another more than her.

This suggests that Akhmatova's idiom was a product of something less graspable than an astute stylistic calculation and leaves us with the necessity of upgrading the second part of Buffone's famous equation to the notion of "self."

Apart from the general sacred aspects of the said entity, its uniqueness in the case of Akhmatova was further secured by her actual physical beauty. She looked positively stunning. Five feet eleven, dark-haired, fair-skinned, with pale grey-green eyes like those of snow leopards, slim and incredibly lithe, she was for a half of a century sketched, painted, cast, carved and photographed by a multitude of artists starting with Amadeo Modigliani. As for the poems dedicated to her, they'd make more volumes than her own collected works.

All this goes to say that the visible part of that self was quite breathtaking; as for the hidden one being a perfect match, there is testimony to it in the form of her writing that blends both.

This blend's chief characteristics are nobility and restraint. Akhmatova is the poet of strict meters, exact rhymes and short sentences. Her syntax is simple and free of subordinate clauses whose gnomic convolutions are responsible for most of Russian literature; in fact, in its simplicity, her syntax resembles English. From the very threshold of her career to its very end she was always perfectly clear and coherent. Among her contemporaries, she is a Jane Austen. In any case, if her sayings were dark, it wasn't due to her grammar.

In the era marked by so much technical experimentation in poetry, she was blatantly non-avant-garde. If anything, her means were visually similar to what prompted that wave of innovations in Russian poetry like everywhere else at the turn of the century: to the Symbolists' quatrains ubiquitous as grass. Yet this visual resemblance was maintained by Akhmatova deliberately: through it she sought not the simplification of her task but a worsening of the odds. She simply wanted to play the game straight, without bending or inventing the rules. In short, she wanted her verse to maintain appearances.

Nothing reveals a poet's weaknesses like classic verse, and that's why it's so universally dodged. To make a couple of lines sound unpredictable without producing a comic effect or echoing someone else is an extremely perplexing affair. This echo aspect of strict meters is most nagging, and no amount of oversaturating the line with concrete physical detail sets one free. Akhmatova sounds so independent because from the very threshold she knew how to exploit the enemy.

She did it by a collage-like diversification of the content. Often within just one stanza she'd cover a variety of seemingly unrelated things. When a person talks in the same breath about the gravity of her emotion, gooseberry blossoms, and pulling the left-hand glove onto her right hand—that compromises the breath—which is, in the poem, its meter—to the degree that one forgets about its pedigree. The echo, in other words, gets subordinated to the discrepancy of objects and in effect provides them with a common denominator; it ceases to be a form and becomes a norm of locution.

Sooner or later this always happens to the echo as

well as to the diversity of things themselves—in Russian verse it was done by Akhmatova, more exactly by that self which bore her name. One can't help thinking that while the inner part of it hears what, by means of rhyme, the language itself suggests about the proximity of those disparate objects, the outer one literally sees from the vantage point of her actual height. She simply couples what has been already bound: in the language and in the circumstances of her life, if not, as they say, in heaven.

Hence the nobility of her diction for she doesn't lay claim to her discoveries. Her rhymes are not assertive, the meter is not insistent. Sometimes she'd drop a syllable or two in a stanza's last or penultimate line in order to create an effect of a choked throat or that of unwitting awkwardness caused by emotional tension. But that would be as far as she'd go for she felt very much at home within the confines of classical verse, thereby suggesting that her raptures and revelations don't require an extraordinary formal treatment, that they are not any greater than those of her predecessors who used these meters before.

This, of course, wasn't exactly true. No one absorbs the past as thoroughly as a poet, if only out of fear of inventing the already invented. (This is why, by the way, a poet is so often regarded as being ''ahead of his time'' which keeps itself busy rehashing clichés.) So no matter what a poet may plan to say, at the moment of speech he always knows that he inherits the subject. The great literature of the past humbles one not only through its quality but through its topical precedence also. The reason why a good poet speaks of his own grief with restraint is that as regards grief he is a Wandering Jew. In this sense, Akhmatova was very much a product of the Petersburg tradition in Russian poetry, the founders of which, in their own turn, had behind them European classicism as well as its Roman and Greek origins. In addition, they too were aristocrats.

If Akhmatova was reticent, it was at least partly because she was carrying the heritage of her predecessors into the Art of this century. This obviously was but an homage to them since it was precisely that heritage which made her this century's poet. She simply regarded herself with her raptures and revelations as a postscript to their message, to what they recorded about their lives. The lives were tragic, and so was the message. If the postscript looks dark, it's because the message was absorbed fully. If she never screams or showers her head with ashes, it's because they didn't.

Such were the cue and the key with which she started. Her first collections were tremendously successful with both the critics and the public. In general, the response to a poet's work should be considered last for it is the last consideration. However, Akhmatova's success was in this respect remarkable if one takes into account its timing, especially in the case of her second and third volumes: 1914 (the outbreak of World War I) and 1917 (the October Revolution in Russia). On the other hand, perhaps it was precisely this deafening background thunder of world events that rendered the private tremolo of this young poet all the more discernible and necessary. In that case again the beginning of this poetic career contained the prophecy of the course it came to run for half a century. What increases the sense of prophecy is that for a Russian ear at the time the thunder of world events was compounded by the incessant and quite meaningless mumbling of the Symbolists. Eventually these two noises shrunk and merged into the threatening incoherent drone of the new era against which she was destined to speak for the rest of her life.

Those early collections ("Evening," "Beads," and "White Flock") dealt mostly with the sentiment which is *de rigueur* of early collections; with that of love. The poems in those books had a diarylike intimacy and immediacy; they'd describe no more than one actual or psychological event and were short—16 to 20 lines at best. As such they could be committed to memory in a flash, and indeed they were—and still are—by generations and generations of Russians.

Still, it was neither their compactness nor subject matter that made one's memory desire to appropriate them; those fixtures were quite familiar to an experienced reader. The news came in the form of a sensibility which manifested itself in the author's treatment of her theme. Betrayed, tormented either by jealousy or guilt, the wounded heroine of these poems speaks more frequently in self-reproach than in anger, forgives more eloquently than accuses, prays rather than screams. She displays all the emotional subtlety and psychological complexity of nineteenth-century Russian prose and all the dignity that the poetry of the same century taught her. Apart from these, there is also a great deal of irony and detachment which are strictly her own and products of her metaphysics rather than shortcuts to resignation.

Needless to say, for her readership those qualities seem to come in both handy and timely. More than any other art, poetry is a form of sentimental education, and the lines the Akhmatova readers learned by heart were to temper their heart against the new era's onslaught of vulgarity. The comprehension of the metaphysics of personal drama betters one's chances of weathering the drama of history. This is why, and not because of the epigrammatic beauty of her lines only, the public clung to them so unwittingly. It was an instinctive reaction; the instinct being that of self-preservation, for the stampede of history was getting more and more audible.

Akhmatova in any case heard it quite clearly. The intensely personal lyricism of "White Flock" is tinged with the note that was destined to become her imprimatur: the note of controlled terror. The mechanism designed to keep in check emotions of a romantic nature proved to be as effective when applied to mortal fears. The latter was increasingly intertwined with the former until they resulted in emotional tautology, and "White Flock" marks the beginning of this process. With this collection, Russian poetry hit "the real, non-calendar twentieth century" but didn't disintegrate at impact.

Akhmatova, to say the least, seemed better prepared for this encounter than most of her contemporaries. Besides, by the time of the Revolution she was twenty-eight years old: that is, neither too young to believe in it nor too old to justify it. Furthermore, she was a woman, and it would be equally unseemly for her to extol or condemn the event. Nor did she decide to accept the change of social order as an invitation to loosen her meter and associative chains. For art doesn't imitate life if only for fear of clichés. She remained true to her diction, to its private timbre, to refracting rather than reflecting life through the prism of the individual heart. Except that the choice of detail whose role in a poem previously was to shift attention from an emotionally pregnant issue presently began to be less and less of a solace, overshadowing the issue itself.

She didn't reject the Revolution: a defiant pose wasn't for her either. Using latter-day locution, she internalized it. She simply took it for what it was: a terrible national upheaval which meant a tremendous increase of grief per individual. She understood this not only because her own share went too high but first and foremost through her very craft. The poet is a born democrat not thanks to the precariousness of his position only but because he caters to the entire nation and employs its language. So does tragedy, and hence their affinity. Akhmatova, whose verse always gravitated to the vernacular, to the idiom of folk song, could identify with the people more thoroughly than those who were pushing at the time their literary or other aims: she simply recognized grief.

Moreover, to say that she identified with the people is to introduce a rationalization which never took place because of an inevitable redundancy. She was a part of the whole, and the pseudonym just furthered her class anonymity. In addition, she always disdained the air of superiority present in the word "poet." "I don't understand these big words," she used to say, "poet, billiard." This wasn't humility; this was the result of the sober perspective in which she kept her existence. The very persistence of love as the theme of her poetry indicates her proximity to the average person. If she differed from her public it was in that her ethics weren't subject to historical adjustment.

Other than that, she was like everybody else. Besides, the time itself didn't allow for great variety. If her poems weren't exactly the vox populi, it's because a nation never speaks with one voice. But neither was her voice that of the *crème de la crème* if only because it was totally devoid of populist nostalgia so peculiar to the Russian intelligentsia. The "we" that she starts to use about this time in self-defense against the impersonality of pain inflicted by History was broadened to this pronoun's linguistic limits not by herself but by the rest of these language speakers. Because of the quality of the future, this "we" was there to stay and the authority of its user to grow.

In any case, there is no psychological difference between Akhmatova's "civic" poems of the World War I and the Revolutionary period and those written a good thirty years later during World War II. Indeed, without the date underneath them, poems like "Prayer" could be attributed to virtually any moment of Russian history in this century, which justifies that particular poem's title. Apart from the sensitivity of her membrane though, this proves that the quality of history for the last eighty years has somewhat simplified the poet's job. It did so to the degree that a poet would spurn a line containing a prophetic possibility and prefer a plain description of a fact or a sensation.

Hence the nominative character of Akhmatova's lines in general and at that period in particular. She knew not only that the emotions and perceptions she dealt with were fairly common but also that time, true to its repetitive nature, would render them universal. She sensed that, like its objects, history has very limited options. What was more important, however, was that those "civic" poems were but fractions borne by her general lyrical current which made their "we" practically indistinguishable from its more frequent, emotionally charged "I." Because of their overlapping, both pronouns were gaining in verisimilitude. Since the name of the current was "love," the poems about the homeland and the epoch were shot through with almost inappropriate intimacy; similarly those about sentiment itself were acquiring an epic timbre. The latter meant the current's widening.

Later in her life, Akhmatova always resented attempts by critics and scholars to confine her significance to her love poetry of the teens of the century. She was perfectly right because the output of the subsequent forty years outweighs her first decade both numerically and qualitatively. Still, one can understand those scholars and critics since after 1922 until her death in 1965 Akhmatova simply couldn't publish a book of her own and they were forced to deal just with what was available. Yet perhaps there was another reason less obvious or less comprehended by those scholars and critics that drew them to the early Akhmatova.

Throughout one's life, Time addresses man in a variety of languages: in those of innocence, love, faith, experience, history, fatigue, cynicism, guilt, decay, etc. Of those, the language of love is clearly the lingua franca. Its vocabulary absorbs all the other tongues, and its utterance gratifies a subject, however inanimate it may be. Also, by being thus uttered, a subject acquires an ecclesiastical, almost sacred denomination, echoing both the way we perceive the objects of our passions and the Good Book's suggestion as to what God is. Love is essentially an attitude maintained by the infinite towards the finite. The reversal constitutes either faith or poetry.

Akhmatova's love poems naturally were in the first place just poems. Apart from anything else, they had a terrific novelistic quality, and a reader could have had a wonderful time explicating the various tribulations and trials of their heroine. (Some did just that, and on the basis of those poems, the heated public imagination would have their author "romantically involved" with Alexander Blok—the poet of the period—as well as with His Imperial Majesty although she was a far better poet than the former and a good six inches taller than the latter.) Half self-portrait, half mask, their poetic persona would aggravate an actual drama with the fatality of theater thus probing both her own and pain's possible limits. Happier states would be subjected to the same query. Realism, in short, was employed as the means of transportation to a metaphysical destination. Still, all this would have amounted to animating the genre's tradition were it not for the sheer quantity of poems dealing with the said sentiment.

That quantity denies both biographical and Freudian approaches for it overshoots the addressees' concreteness and renders them as pretexts for the author's speech. What art and sexuality have in common is that both are sublimations of one's creative energy, that denies them hierarchy. The nearly idiosyncratic persistence of the early Akhmatova love poems suggests not so much the recurrence of passion as the frequency of prayer. Correspondingly, different though their imagined or real protagonists are, these poems display a considerable stylistic similarity because love as content is in the habit of limiting formal patterns. The same goes for faith. After all, there are only so many adequate manifestations for truly strong sentiments; which, in the end, is what explains rituals.

It is the finite's nostalgia for the infinite that accounts for the recurrence of the love theme in Akhmatova's verse, not the actual entanglements. Love indeed has become for her a language, a code to record Time's messages or at least, to convey their tune; she simply heard them better this way. For what interested this poet most was not her own life but precisely Time and the effects of its monotone on the human psyche and on her own diction in particular. If she later resented attempts to reduce her to her early writing, it was not because she disliked the status of the habitually lovesick girl: it was because her diction and with it, the code, changed subsequently a lot in order to make the monotone of the infinite more audible.

In fact, it was already quite distinct in "Anno Domini MCMXXI"—her fifth and technically speaking last collection. In some of its poems, that monotone merges with the author's voice to the point that she has to sharpen the concreteness of detail or image in order to save them, and by the same token her own mind, from the inhuman neutrality of the meter. Their fusion, or rather the former's subordination to the latter, came later. In the meantime, she was trying to save her own notions of existence from being overtaken by those supplied to her by prosody: for prosody knows more about Time than a human being would like to reckon with.

Close exposure to this knowledge, or more accurately to this memory of Time restructured, results in an inordinately mental acceleration that robs insights that come from actual reality of their novelty, if not of their gravity. No poet can ever close this gap, but a conscientious one may lower his pitch or muffle his diction so as to downplay his estrangement from real life. This is done sometimes for purely aesthetic purposes: to make one's voice less theatrical, less bel-canto-like. More frequently though the purpose of this camouflage is, again, to retain sanity, and Akhmatova, a poet of strict meters, was using it precisely to that end. But the more she did so, the more inexorably her voice was approaching the impersonal tonality of Time itself until they merged into something that makes one shudder trying to guess—as in her "Northern Elegies"—who is it there, hiding behind the pronoun "I"?

What happened to pronouns was happening to other parts of speech which would peter out or loom large in the perspective of Time supplied by prosody. Akhmatova was a very concrete poet, but the more concrete the image the more extemporary it would become because of the accompanying meter. No poem is ever written for its story-line sake only, like no life is lived for the sake of an obituary. What is called the music of a poem is essentially restructured in such a way that it brings this poem's content into a linguistically inevitable, memorable focus.

Sound, in other words, is the seat of Time in the poem, a background against which its content acquires a stereoscopic quality. The power of Akhmatova's lines comes from her ability to convey the music's impersonal epic sweep which more than matched their poetic content, especially from the Twenties on. The effect of her instrumentation upon her themes was akin to that of somebody used to being put against the wall suddenly being put against the horizon.

The above should be kept very much in mind by the foreign reader of Akhmatova since that horizon vanishes in translations, leaving on the page absorbing but one-dimensional content. On the other hand, the foreign reader may perhaps be consoled by the fact that this poet's native audience also has been forced to deal with her work in a very misrepresented fashion. What translation has in common with censorship is that both operate on the basis of the "what's possible" principle, and it must be noted that linguistic barriers can be as high as those erected by the state. Akhmatova, in any case, is surrounded by both and it's only the former that shows signs of crumbling.

"Anno Domini MCMXXI" was her last collection: in the forty-four years that followed she had no book of her own. In the postwar period there were technically speaking two slim editions of her work, consisting mainly of a few reprinted early lyrics plus genuinely patriotic war poems and doggerel bits extolling the arrival of peace. These last ones were written by her in order to win the release of her son from the labor camps in which he nonetheless spent eighteen years. These publications in no way can be regarded as her own for the poems were selected by the editors of the state-run publishing house and their aim was to convince the public (especially those abroad) that Akhmatova was alive, well and loyal. They totaled some fifty pieces and had nothing in common with her output during those four decades.

For a poet of Akhmatova's stature this meant being buried alive, with a couple of slabs marking the grave. Her going under was a product of several forces, mostly that of history whose chief element is vulgarity and whose immediate agent is the state. Now, by MCMXXI which means 1921, the new state could already be at odds with Akhmatova, whose first husband, poet Nikolai Gumiliov, was executed by its security forces, allegedly the direct order of the state's head, Vladimir Lenin. A spin off of a didactic, eye-for-eye mentality, the new state could expect from Akhmatova nothing but retaliation, especially given her reputed tendency for an autobiographic touch.

Such was, presumably, the state's logic, furthered by the destruction in the subsequent decade and a half of her entire circle (including her closest friends, poets Vladimir Narbut and Osip Mandelstam). It culminated in the arrests of her son, Lev Gumiliov, and her third husband, art-historian Nikolai Punin, who soon died in prison. Then came World War II.

Those fifteen years preceding the war were perhaps the darkest in the whole of Russian history; undoubtedly so they were in Akhmatova's own life. It's the material which this period supplied, or more accurately the lives it subtracted, that made her eventually earn the title of the Muse of Wailing. It simply replaced the frequency of poems about love with that of poems in memoriam. Death which she would previously evoke as a solution for this or that emotional tension became too real for any emotion to matter. From a figure of speech it became a figure that leaves you speechless.

If she proceeded to write, it's because parody absorbs death, and because she felt guilty that she survived. The pieces that constitute her "Wreath for the Dead" are simply attempts to let those whom she outlived absorb or at least join prosody. It's not that she tried to "immortalize" her dead: most of them were the pride of Russian literature already and thus had immortalized themselves enough. She simply tried to manage the meaninglessness of existence which suddenly gaped before her because of the destruction of its meaning's sources, to domesticate the reprehensible infinity by inhabiting it with familiar shadows. Besides, addressing the dead was the only way of preventing speech from slipping into a howl.

The elements of howl, however, are quite audible in other of Akhmatova's poems of the period and later. They'd appear in a form either of idiosyncratic excessive rhyming or as a nonsequitur line interjected in an otherwise coherent narrative. Nevertheless, the poems dealing directly with someone's death are free of anything of this sort, as though the author doesn't want to offend her addressees with her emotional extremities. This refusal to exploit the ultimate opportunity to impose herself upon them echoes, of course, the practice of her lyric poetry. But by continuing to address the dead as though they were alive, by not adjusting her diction to "the occasion," she also refuses the opportunity to exploit the dead as those ideal, absolute inter-locutors that every poet seeks and finds either in the dead or among angels.

As a theme, death is a good litmus test for a poet's ethics. The "in memoriam" genre is frequently used to excercise self-pity or for metaphysical trips that denote the subconscious superiority of survivor over victim, of majority (of the alive) over minority (of the dead). Akhmatova would have none of that. She particularizes her fallen instead of generalizing about them since she writes for a minority with which it's easier for her to identify in any case. She simply continues to treat them as individuals whom she knew and who she senses wouldn't like to be used as the point of departure for no matter how spectacular a destination.

Naturally enough, poems of this sort couldn't be published, nor could they even be written down or retyped. They could only be memorized by the author and by some seven other people since she didn't trust her own memory. From time to time, she'd meet a person privately and would ask him or her to recite quietly this or that selection as a means of inventory. This precaution was far from being excessive: people would disappear forever for smaller things than a piece of paper with a few lines on it. Besides, she feared not so much for her own life as for her son's who was in a camp and whose release she desperately tried to obtain for eighteen years. A little piece of paper with a few lines on it could cost a lot, and more to him than to her who could lose only hope and, perhaps, mind.

The days of both, however, would have been numbered had the authorities found her "Requiem," a cycle of poems describing an ordeal of a woman whose son is arrested and who waits under prison walls with a parcel for him and scurries about the thresholds of state's offices to find out about his fate. Now, this time around she was autobiographical indeed, yet the power of "Requiem" lies in the fact that Akhmatova's biography was too common. This Requiem mourns the mourners: mothers losing sons, wives turning widows, sometimes both as was the author's case. This is a tragedy where the choir perishes before the hero.

The degree of compassion with which the various voices of this "Requiem" are rendered can be explained only by the author's Orthodox faith; the degree of understanding and forgiveness which accounts for this work's piercing, almost unbearable lyricism, only by the uniqueness of her heart, her self and this self's sense of Time. No creed would help to understand, much less forgive, let alone survive this double widowhood at the hands of the regime, this fate of her son, these forty years of being silenced and ostracized. No Anna Gorenko would be able to take it. Anna Akhmatova did, and it's as though she knew what there was in store when she took this pen name.

At certain periods of history it is only poetry that is capable of dealing with reality by condensing it into something graspable, something that otherwise couldn't be retained by the mind. In that sense, the whole nation took up the pen name of Akhmatova—which explains her popularity and which, more importantly enabled her to speak for the nation as well as to tell it something it didn't know. She was, essentially, a poet of human ties: cherished, strained, severed. She showed these evolutions first through the prism of the individual heart, then through the prism of history, such as it was. This is about as much as one gets in the way of optics anyway.

These two perspectives were brought into sharp focus through prosody which is simply a repository of Time within language. Hence, by the way, her ability to forgive—because forgiveness is not a virtue postulated by creed but a property of time in both its mundane and metaphysical senses. This is also why her verses are to survive whether published or not: because of the prosody, because they are charged with time in both said senses. They will survive because language is older than state and because prosody always survives history. In fact, it hardly needs history; all it needs is a poet, and Akhmatova was just that.

—JOSEPH BRODSKY

ANNA AKHMATOVA
Poems

WHILE READING HAMLET

A dust-covered patch to the right of the cemetery.
Beyond that, a river of unfolding blue.
"Get thee to a nunnery," you said, "Or marry
An idiot—It's up to you."

That's the sort of thing princes always say,
But I won't forget it as I grow older.
May your words keep flowing as centuries wear away,
Like an ermine mantle tossed over someone's shoulder.

1909

The three things he loved most in life
Were white peacocks, music at mass,
And tattered maps of America.
He didn't like kids who cried and he
Didn't like raspberry jam with tea
Or womanish hysteria.
. . . And I was, like it or not, his wife.

1910–1911

THE SONG OF THE FINAL MEETING

My breast was bound with a cold band,
And still my steps were light.
The glove intended for my left hand,
I put upon my right.

At the thought of the stairs, I grew faint-hearted,
But I knew, there were only three!
An autumnal whisper in the maples started
Begging: "Die with me!

"Fate cheated me—fate, so abysmal,
So moody and full of spite . . ."
I answered: "My dear! I too am dismal.
I'll die with you tonight . . ."

The final meeting: I stood on the road.
The house was as dark as shame.
Only, in the bedroom, candles showed
An indifferent yellow flame.

1911

A ruddy youth wandered forlornly around,
In and out the alleys of trees on the shore.
A century passes, we still hear the sound—
Footsteps rustle on the forest floor.
The pine needles' thick and bristling mat
Carpets the stub of each fallen tree.
Here's where he put his three-cornered hat
And a rumpled book of poems by Parny.

1911

This poem is a tribute to Alexander Pushkin, 1799–1837, regarded as the greatest Russian poet, one of the four or five best poets in postmedieval Europe.

Parny: E. D. De Forger, 1753–1814, a French poet.

Memories of the sun fade as my heart grows numb—
The grass is yellower, too.
The wind toys with what snowflakes have already
come—
So few, so few.

In narrow canals, there's already nothing that flows—
Water stands still.
Nothing ever happens here, nothing grows—
It never will!

Against the sky, the willow lifts its skeletal life,
Its see-through shawl.
Maybe it's better that I'm not your wife,
After all.

Memories of the sun fade as my heart grows numb.
What's this? Darkness in town?
Maybe! And during the night, winter may come—
And settle down.

1911

5

I pressed my hands together under cover
Of my veil. "Why are you so pale today?"
—Because I intoxicated my lover
With numbing anguish, and drove him away.

How could I forget? He went out, reeling.
His mouth dreadful—twisted, grim . . .
I ran down the stairs, not touching the railing,
At the gate I caught up with him.

I shouted hoarsely—"It was just a joke.
You mustn't leave me—I'd rather be dead."
He smiled calmly, terribly, then he spoke:
"Don't stand out here in the wind," he said.

1911

As if through a straw, you drink my soul.
I know—It's bitter and intoxicating. I won't seek
Any mercy, won't interrupt the torture. No,
My calm will endure for another week.

When you're finished, tell me. It's probably good
That my soul isn't anywhere it can be found.
I'll walk down the path and stand where I stood
And watch the children at play in the playground.

Every gooseberry bush has a flowery cover.
They're trundling bricks beyond my fence.
Who are you anyway, my brother or lover?
I don't know. I don't have to. It makes no difference.

How light it is here, and how unfriendly.
My tired body has given way—
It's at rest. And passersby think vaguely:
She probably was widowed yesterday.

1911

I live like a cuckoo in a clock,
I don't envy the birds of a flock.
They wind me up, and I cuckoo.
A fate like this—sad but true—
I can only wish, and do,
On an enemy or two.

1911

They didn't bring me a letter today:
He forgot, or went on one of his trips;
Spring's the trill of silver laughter on the lips,
I see the boats in the harbor sway.
They didn't bring me a letter today . . .

Not long ago he was with me still,
Expressly enamored, amorous, and mine,
But that was when winter gave off a white shine,
Now it's spring and the sadness of spring can kill,
Not long ago he was with me still . . .

I listen: a light, trembling blow strikes home,
It beats, beats, as if premortal pain were cause,
Now I fear my heart will break its bonds like laws
Before I can finish this tender poem . . .

1911

OVER THE WATER

Slender shepherd boy, don't laugh,
Someone's crazy, I know who.
I recall both cape and staff,
Recall with rue.
If I stood, I'd fall—that wouldn't do,
Tootles the shepherd's pipe: too-too!

As if in a dream, we said farewell,
I whispered, "I'll see it through."
He laughed and answered, "Just as well:
In hell, we'll no doubt meet anew."
If I stood, I'd fall—that wouldn't do,
Tootles the shepherd's pipe: too-too!

Oh millpond, deep as tomorrow,
Staining my reflections blue,
It won't be from shame or sorrow
That I'll come to you.
I'll fall soundless, as if on cue,
And far away a pipe will play: too-too.

1911

A doer of nothing, I came here—Why not?
It's all the same to me where I am bored.
A gristmill dozes on this hilly spot.
You can live here for years and not say a word.

Gently, a bee begins to row
Past the dried-out morning glory bed
By the pond I call "mermaid" although
The mermaid in question is, of course, dead.

The pond has rusty scum on it now,
Its wide surface is covered with slime,
Over each quaking aspen bough
The brilliant moon began to shine.

The poplars give off a damp smell.
I notice it all as if it were new.
I say nothing and am ready, as well,
Earth, to become, once again, you.

1911

FISHERMAN

Above the elbow, your arms are bare,
And your eyes are bluer than ice.
The pungent, stifling smell of tar
Is like your tan, exceedingly nice.

The collar of your sky-blue coat
Is always, always, open wide,
They gasp, the maidens, taking note
And start to blush, or hide.

Even the kid who goes into town
Selling her smelt for about what they cost,
In the evening wanders down
To the pier as if she were lost.

Her arms are weak, her cheeks are pale,
Her exhausted look is mysterious and
Crabs tickle her feet without fail
As they crawl out on the sand.

But she doesn't catch them any more,
Her outstretched hands are no longer discerning.
The blood beats faster in her body's core,
The body wounded now by yearning.

1911

Pusscat, watch out, an embroidered owl
Scowls from a pillow on the bed,
Gray Miss Pusscat, please don't growl,
Granddad will hear what you just said.
Nanny, this candle isn't lit,
Mice can nibble me if they try.
That dratted owl, I'm afraid of it,
Who embroidered him and why?

1911

MASQUERADE IN THE PARK

The moonlight reaches under the eaves,
Its course across the river is erratic . . .
The small cold hands of the marquise
Are lightly aromatic.

"O prince!"—She smiles and gives a curtsy,
Languidly turns pale beneath her mask—
"In the quadrille you're our vis-à-vis"—
With fiery thoughts of what love could ask.

The door's hid by poplars, gray as opal
And by low-hanging hops as well.
"Baghdad or Constantinople
I will conquer for you, ma belle!"

"One fears to embrace you, marquise,
There's seldom a smile in your glance!"
It's dark and cool under the trees,
"Well, all right! why shouldn't we dance?"

They walk out slowly to the place
Colored lights ring elm and maple trunks,
In green costumes trimmed with lace
Two ladies are wagering with monks.

And then they meet with merriment—
He holds azaleas, pale Pierrot:
"The marquise's hat-feather is bent,
My prince! *You* couldn't have done it, I know."

1911

Wine-dark grapes smell sweet here . . .
Inebriating distances poke fun.
Your voice is muffled and devoid of cheer.
I don't feel sorry for anyone.

Between the grapes spider nets quiver,
The supple vines are as thin as ever,
Clouds float by like chunks of ice that shiver
The bright waters of a blue river.

The sun in the sky. The sun shines like new.
Tell that wave about the pain in all this.
Oh, surely she will answer you.
Perhaps she will even give you a kiss.

1911

IN THE WOODS

Four eyes shine—four diamonds,
My two and the owl's two overhead.
How terrible is the tale that ends
With the death of my beloved.

My words ring out, senseless and mordant,
I'm lying in the grass, damp and green,
And from above, looking oh so important,
The owl listens, quiet and keen.

We're surrounded by firs that tighten our breath,
The sky, a black square, continues to hover,
You know, don't you, about his death,
He was killed by my elder brother—

It wasn't in war or its aftermath,
It wasn't in combat or bloody strife,
But coming to see me on a forest path
That my lover lost his life.

1911

TO THE MUSE

My Muse-sister kept on looking
At me: her gaze was clear and shining.
She took away my golden ring,
The gift that had signaled the start of spring.

Muse! See how happy they feel—
Girls and women, and widows—See?
I'd rather die on the torturer's wheel
Than endure these fetters made for me.

I know: I too will have to turn
To telling my fortune by tearing apart
A daisy. Everyone must learn
To endure love's torture in his heart.

I burn a candle in the window
Till dawn. There's no one at all I miss.
But I don't, don't, don't want to know.
Who's enjoying whose kiss.

Tomorrow, mirrors will sneer: "We're not fond
Of your gaze—It's not clear or shining," they'll say.
To which I'll quietly respond:
"She took God's gift away."

1912

17

I learned a simple and wise existence,
I learned to look at the sky and pray,
And in the evening to walk a good distance,
Walking unneeded worries away.

When ravines rustle and burdock roams
And yellow-berried rowans are in their glory,
I put together light-hearted poems
About life, ephemeral, transitory.

I return. The fluffy cat doesn't glower:
He licks my palm and purrs long and hard,
And a light comes on in the little tower
Of a nearby lakeside lumberyard.

Sometimes there's sound for a moment or more—
The cry of a stork on the house or near it.
—And if you should happen to knock on my door,
I very much doubt if I would hear it.

1912

As I die, I long for immortality.
The cloud of dust is low in which . . .
Naked red devils let it be,
Even a caldron of foul-smelling pitch.

Tell lies while crawling, thick and fast,
You forking threats from books gone hoary.
Only let my memory last,
Only don't take away my memory.

If in the journey to that stronghold,
His face only will not seem strange,
I'm ready to pay a hundredfold
For the smiles and dreams we used to exchange.

The deadly hour will offer me
Poison to drink—I won't have a choice.
People will come, and help to bury
Both my body and my voice.

1912

My voice is weak, my will doesn't weaken though,
I feel even better without love.
Heaven is high, mountain breezes blow,
And my thoughts are as chaste as the sky above.

My nurse-insomnia is elsewhere and
Gray ashes do not chill me to the marrow,
The tower clock's terribly crooked hand
No longer looks to me like a deadly arrow.

How quickly the past is losing its grip on my heart!
Deliverance is near. I'll forgive everything,
As I watch a sunbeam settle down and start
To caress the green ivy, dewy with spring.

1912

The smell of inanimate things and flowers
Is pleasant in this pleasant home.
In the orchard, by beds and bowers,
Mounds of bright vegetables lie on the loam.

The air's still cool but they weren't afraid,
They uncovered the hothouses yesterday.
There's a little pond, about which I'll say
Just that its slime looks like green brocade.

A little boy, frightened, as if on a dare,
Told me with an excitement that carried,
That a giant carp is living in there
Along with the lady carp he married.

1913

21

I see on the customs house a faded flag.
A yellow murk hangs over the city, not high.
My heart is beating as if caught on a snag—
It stands still and now it's painful for me to sigh.

If only I could again be a peasant girl
I'd go for a shoe- or sock-less walk on the shore,
I'd arrange my hair on my head with a crowning curl,
And sing in an excited voice once more.

I'd again, at the Kherson church, keep looking down,
I'd look at those swarthy domes from my balcony,
And not know that from gladness and renown,
Hearts grow old irrevocably.

1913

Around my neck are rosary strands,
My eyes cannot focus, though open and dry,
In a furry muff I hide my hands,
My eyes are no longer able to cry.

And the face seems paler than of late,
Because of the silky violet dress
And the uncurled bangs hang down straight
To the line of my eyebrows, more or less.

This slow walk makes the picture complete,
It won't resemble flight any more,
It's as if a raft were under my feet,
And not the squares of a parquet floor.

The pale lips are slightly parted,
The breathing is ragged, as if from a race.
On my breast the flowers' trembling has started,
Bouquet from a meeting that never took place.

1913

We're heavy drinkers here, and women of loose
    morals—
How unhappy all of us are in our crowd.
Flowers and birds all over the walls
Are languishing for lack of a cloud.

There's a little puff of smoke, a rope
Of smoke over your black pipe.
I'm wearing a tight skirt in the hope
Of appearing a svelte, elegant type.

The windows have been forever nailed shut.
What's it like outside—Is it raining or snowing?
Your eyes are not just cautious, but
Cat eyes, cautious both coming and going.

Oh, how my heart is languishing—
Could I be waiting for my death knell?
And that girl over there who's dancing—
No doubt about it, she'll end in hell.

1913

Earthly fame's like smoke, I guess—
It's not what I asked for from those above.
I brought so much luck and happiness
To all the men I blessed with love.
One's alive even at this date,
Mad for a girlfriend he met somewhere.
The other turned bronze and stands in wait
Covered with snow, in the village square.

1914

Broad and yellow is the evening light,
The coolness of April is dear.
You, of course, are several years late,
Even so, I'm happy you're here.

Sit close at hand and look at me,
With those eyes, so cheerful and mild:
This blue notebook is full, you see,
Full of poems I wrote as a child.

Forgive me, forgive me, for having grieved
For ignoring the sunlight, too.
And especially for having believed
That so many others were you.

1915

There's a sacred limit to any closeness,
Even the passionate fact can't transcend,
Though in fearful silence lips on lips may press
And the heart love tears to pieces won't mend.

And friendship is powerless and years
Of intense high-minded happiness,
Where the soul is free, a stranger to fears
Of the slow languors of passionate excess.

Those who strive to reach it play the part
Of madness, those who succeed are stricken—And
Now you understand why my heart
Is not beating beneath your hand.

1915

The loss of true feelings and words renders us
Actors gone deaf or painters gone blind,
It's the same loss when women find
Time has made them no longer gorgeous.

But do not try to keep or protect
That which was given to you from heaven:
We know we're supposed to be like leaven—
We're condemned to squander, not to collect.

So walk alone, and heal the blind,
That in the difficult hour of doubt
You may see your disciples mock and gloat,
And note the indifference of the crowd.

1915

PRAYER

Give me illness for years on end,
Shortness of breath, insomnia, fever.
Take away my child and friend,
The gift of song, my last believer.
I pray according to Your rite,
After many wearisome days,—
That the storm cloud over Russia might
Turn white and bask in a glory of rays.

1915

Like a white stone in the depths of a well,
One memory glimmers deep within my soul.
I can't, I don't want to fight its spell,
Joy and pain together make up its whole.

It always seems to me that he who looks
Deep in my eyes will see it without fail,
Become more thoughtful, sadder than in books,
Than someone listening to a mournful tale.

For gods, I know, it's not a great endeavor,
Turning people to things for easy glory.
So that wondrous sadness may live forever,
You've been turned into my memory.

1916

SONG ABOUT SONGS

It will burn you at the start,
As if to breezes you were bare,
Then drop deep into your heart
Like a single salty tear.

And a heart full of spite
Will come to know regret.
And this sorrow, although light,
It will not forget.

Others will reap. I only sow.
Of course! When the triumphant horde
Of scythers lays the grain low,
Bless them, O Lord!

And so that I may lift
My eyes in thanks to You above,
Let me give the world a gift
More incorruptible than love.

1916

You can look straight into my room—
I didn't hang a single drape.
The reason today is free from gloom
Is that I know you can't escape.
Cite the codes I couldn't keep,
Spitefully deride my folly.
I was the reason you couldn't sleep,
I was your melancholy.

1916

It seems that the voice we humans own
Will never sound, never celebrate,
Only a wind from the age of stone
Keeps on knocking at the black gate.
And it seems to me that under the sun
I alone remain—this honor's mine,
Simply because I was the first
Who wanted to drink the deadly wine.

1917

As for saying goodbye, we don't know how,
Shoulder to shoulder we keep on walking.
Its getting darker and darker now,
You are pensive, and I'm not talking.

We enter a church—Inside they believe
In funerals, christenings, weddings too,
Without looking at each other, we leave . . .
Why is everything different between me and you?

Or else we sit in trampled snow
In a cemetery and begin to sigh,
You take a stick and draw the chateau,
Where we'll always be, just you and I.

1917

34

Late at night. Monday. The twenty-third.
The capital's outlines in the mists.
Some idiot's given us the word,
He's informed the world that love exists.

And out of boredom or laziness
Everyone believes and lives that way:
They all look forward to trysts, no less,
They sing their love songs night and day.

But to some, the secret's revealed,
The smallest silence weighs like a brick . . .
I too stumbled on what was concealed.
Since then I've felt as if I was sick.

1917

On the hard crests of the snowdrifts that lead
To your strange white house, we walk along.
We both quiet down as we proceed,
And, sweeter than the sweetest song,
Is this tender silence between me and you,
Is the catching sway of the rows of firs,
Is for me this delicate dream come true,
The bell-like ringing of your spurs.

1917

Suddenly it was quiet everywhere,
The last of the poppies had blown away.
Frozen in a daydreamy stare,
I met darkness early, coming to stay.

The gates are tightly shut from without,
The night is black, wind doesn't exist.
Where are you, joy? Where care, and doubt?
Where are you, darling—at another tryst?

I didn't find the secret ring.
For days, I waited and guessed.
That tender captive, a song to sing,
Perished inside my breast.

1917

During each day—today, tomorrow—
A vague, disquieting time will arise.
I'll speak quietly with sorrow,
And not even open my sleepy eyes.
She pounds like blood, push to shove,
Like warm breathing, clear and clean,
Or even like a happy love,
Very reasonable and mean.

1917

I hear the oriole's voice, clear and distressed,
I greet the waning of the summer but
One wheat ear against another pressed
The sickles with reptilian hisses cut.

The short hems of the women in the field
Fly in the wind like flags on a holiday.
Now I yearn for the joyful bells that pealed,
His dusty lashes—And he didn't look away.

I don't expect caresses or words to spare
In expectation of that dark descent,
But do come look at the paradises where
Together we were blissful and innocent.

1917

THE TALE OF THE BLACK RING

1

From my grandmama—Tartar, stern—
Gifts were rare, as I would learn.
When my parents christened me,
She railed about it bitterly.
But before her death she changed,
Tried to make us less estranged.
"Oh, I've lived too long!" she'd groan.
"How my granddaughter has grown."
She forgave me everything
And bequeathed me the black ring.
"It suits her, that fiery one,
It will make her have more fun."

2

I told all my suitor-friends:
"Sorrow lasts but joy soon ends."
I left, covering my face:
I'd lost the ring, and knew my place.
My suitor-friends said in despair:
"We looked for your ring everywhere,
By the seashore in the sand,
Among the pines in the meadowland."
And, catching up with me in the lane,
The boldest one, not a little vain,
Said he wanted me to stay
With him till the end of day.
I was surprised that this had happened;
I got angry with my friend
Because his eyes were soft and tender:

"None of you is my defender,
All you do is laugh and boast,
See who's silliest the most,
Bring me flowers night and day."
I told them all to go away.

3

As soon as I came home that day,
I screamed like a bird of prey,
Fell on my bed, began to recall
For the hundredth time the whole of it all:
How I sat at supper, lost in surmise,
Looking into those dark eyes,
Sat at the table and couldn't drink,
At the oaken table, couldn't eat or think,
How under the tablecloth's patterned rim,
I secretly passed the ring to him,
How he looked at me with a look that could scorch,
Got up and walked out, onto the porch.

They'll never find it, I know that today.
Over the fast little boat far away
The sky swirled red by night,
The sails unfurled their white.

1917–1930

I asked a nearby cuckoo to say
How many years I had left to live.
The tops of the pine trees started to sway,
Sunbeams poured down as if through a sieve,
But in the woods, not a sound was heard.
I'm walking homeward now,
And the cool wind, self-assured,
Soothes my fevered brow.

1919

Fear, fingering objects in the dark,
Points a ray of moonlight at the hatchet.
A sound beyond the wall, muffled yet stark—
A ghost? A rat? The door? Did I latch it?

In the kitchen, it splashes water in the sink,
It counts the wobbly floorboards, makes them crack,
Darts past the attic window, quick as a wink,
Wearing a beard that's glossy and black,

And quiets down. It's full of evil zest.
It hid the matches and blew out the candle.
A firing squad—*that* I could handle.
A glittering line of rifles aimed at my chest.

I'd much prefer to lie on an unpainted scaffold,
Hearing the crowd in the green village square moan
Or cry out in joy as if prizes were being raffled,
Then shed my dear red blood until it's gone.

I press a smooth little cross to my breast:
O Lord, let my soul rediscover rest.
A musty odor, sickeningly sweet,
Floats up at me from the cool bedsheet.

1921

I called death down on the heads of those I cherished.
One after the other, their deaths occurred.
I cannot bear to think how many perished.
These graves were all predicted by my word.
As ravens circle above the place
Where they smell fresh-blooded limbs,
So my love, with triumphant face,
Inflicted its wild hymns.

Being with you is sweet beyond mention,
You're as close as the heart I call my own.
Give me both hands, pay careful attention,
I beseech you: go away, leave me alone.
Don't let me know where you make your homes.
Oh, Muse, don't call to him from above,
May he live, unmentioned in my poems,
Ignorant of all my love.

1921

Why are you wandering around so,
Breathless, as if on the run?
Probably you suspect or know
Two souls have been fused into one.

You'll be consoled by me in ways
That still haven't dawned on you.
And if you hurt me with an angry phrase,
You'll be wounded, too.

1922

Beyond the lake, the moon's stopped in space,
It looks like the window, open wide,
Of a hushed house, still and bright inside
Where something terrible's taken place.

Did the lady take a lover and run away,
Did they bring the master home dead tonight,
Or has the little girl vanished from sight
And they've found her shoe down by the bay . . .

You can't tell from earth. We sensed a fate
So awful we fell silent abruptly.
Owls began to hoot a eulogy.
And a hot wind banged on the garden gate.

1922

LOT'S WIFE

And Lot's wife looked back
and became a pillar of salt.

And the just man followed God's ambassador here,
Huge and bright against the mountain black.
But alarm spoke loudly in the woman's ear:
It's not too late, you can still look back

At red-towered Sodom where you were born,
At the square where you sang, where you sat to spin,
At the windows of the high house, forlorn,
Where you bore your beloved husband children.

She looked,—deadly pain found the fault,
Her eyes couldn't see if they saw or not;
And her body became translucent salt,
Her lively feet were rooted to the spot.

She's seen as a kind of loss and yet
Who will grieve for this woman, cry for this wife?
My heart alone will never forget:
For a single look, she gave up her life.

1922–1924

47

THE MUSE

When at night I await the beloved guest,
Life seems to hang by a thread. "What is youth?" I
    demand
Of the room. "What is honor, freedom, the rest,
In the presence of her who holds the flute in her hand?"

But now she is here. Tossing aside her veil,
She considers me. "Are you the one who came
To Dante, who dictated the pages of Hell
To him?" I ask her. She replies, "I am."

1924

If the lunar horror splashes around,
The whole city in poison must steep.
Without any hope of falling asleep,
Through the greenish murk I try to peer,
Not my childhood, not the sea comes clear,
Not the flight butterflies had chosen
Over a bed of snowy narcissus
In nineteen sixteen, more or less . . .
But the round dance, forever frozen,
Of your tall graveyard cypresses.

1928

THE LAST TOAST

I drink to the house, already destroyed,
And my whole life, too awful to tell,
To the loneliness we together enjoyed,
I drink to you as well,
To the eyes with deadly cold imbued,
To the lips that betrayed me with a lie,
To the world for being cruel and rude,
To God who didn't save us, or try.

1934

BORIS PASTERNAK

He who compared himself to the eye of a horse,
Glances, looks, sees, recognizes,
And puddles shine like molten diamonds, of course,
And any ice is lost in surmises.

In the purple mist, unvisited streets unwind,
A station, logs, leaves, doves.
Train whistles, the crunch of watermelon rind,
Shy hands in perfumed suede gloves.

Rumbles, clangs, screeches, reach high tide
And die. This means he's coming: he carefully places
Each foot on pine needles, tries as he's always tried
Not to frighten the light sleep of empty spaces.

This means he's counting grains, keeping a tab
On empty ears of wheat, that he came back,
Again, from someone's funeral to the slab
In the Daryal wilds, which is also accursed and black.

Languor again burns the Moscovian loam,
In the distance, deadly bells jingle. Do you know
Who's gotten lost not even a stone's throw from home,
Where everything ends and you're up to your waist in
    snow?

Because he compared smoke to the Laocoon,
And celebrated thistles in graveyard places,
Because he filled worlds with new ringing and so on
In reflected stanzas original spaces—

He's been rewarded with a kind of eternal childhood,
His keen sight and generosity shine like the sun,
The earth was his inheritance, plain and wildwood,
And he shared it with everyone.

1936

VORONEZH

(*To Osip Mandelstam*)

The city is caught in the grip of ice—
Trees, walls, snow, are as under glass.
Over crystals, I and the patterned sleighs
Go our separate, unsteady ways.
And above St. Peter's steeple—crows,
And poplars—a light-green vault that glows—
Blurred, lackluster, in the sunny dust.
The triumphant landscape blows into thought
This is where Kulikovo was fought.
And the poplars like wineglasses raised in a toast
Suddenly ring out more clearly above us.
As though at a wedding the assembled host
Were drinking our union to show how they love us.
But Fear and the Muse in turn guard the place
Where the banished poet has gone.
And the night that comes with quickened pace
Is ignorant of dawn.

1936

Osip Mandelstam: 1891–1939, noted Russian poet, arrested twice, died in prison.
Kulikovo: great battle against the Tartars, 1378.

DANTE

Il mio bel San Giovanni,

Inferno, Dante

He didn't go back even after he was dead
To that ancient Florence of his.
Leaving, he looked straight ahead:
It's for him I am singing this.
Night. A torch. A final kiss.
Outside, the sound of fate—a kind
Of howl. From hell he sent her a curse.
In paradise, she was still on his mind.
He didn't go barefoot, late at night,
Penitentially attired,
Through Florence—treacherous, full of spite,
Whom he so faithfully desired.

1936

CLEOPATRA

I am air and fire . . .

Shakespeare

The Alexandrian palaces
Were shrouded in sweet shadow.

Pushkin

Already she was kissing the dead Antony's
Lips, and had wept on her knees before Caesar,
    betrayed
By her servants. The evening mist was spread under
    trees
Like cloth. The victorious Roman trumpets brayed,

And the last one to be caught by her beauty, slim
And handsome, whispers in mortification: "It's
    arranged—
You, in his triumph, he'll send like a slave before him."
But the calm arc of the swan's neck is unchanged.

Tomorrow they will chain her children. And yet
She has something left in the world to do—one more
    jest.
And the little black snake, as if a parting regret,
With an equable hand, she puts on her swarthy breast.

1940

THE WILLOW

And a decrepit bunch of trees.

Pushkin

I grew up where all was patterned and silent,
In the cool nursery of the age, itself young;
I didn't like human words, spoken or sung,
But I understood what the wind meant.
I liked burdock and nettles but the willow tree,
The silver willow, I liked especially.
It lived gratefully with me till now
And with its weeping branches seemed
To make dreamlessness like something dreamed.
It's hard to believe I outlived it somehow.
There's a stump. And in alien tongues, other willows
    will
Be saying whatever it is they say
Under our skies, under theirs. I'm completely still.
It's as if my brother had died today.

1940

When a person dies,
His portraits change.
His eyes see differently and his mouth
Smiles different smiles.
I realized this when I came back
From the funeral of a poet.
And I've verified my insight
Many times since then.

1940

IN 1940

1.

When they bury an epoch,
No psalms are read while the coffin settles,
The grave will be adorned with a rock,
With bristly thistles and nettles.
Only the gravediggers dig and fill,
Working with zest. Business to do!
And it's so still, my God, so still,
You can hear time passing by you.
And later, like a corpse, it will rise
Ride the river in spring like a leaf,—
But the son doesn't recognize
His mother, the grandson turns away in grief,
Bowed heads do not embarrass,
Like a pendulum goes the moon.

Well, this is the sort of silent tune
That plays in fallen Paris.

2.   To Londoners

The twenty-fourth drama by William Shakespeare
Time is writing with a careless hand.
Since we partake of the feast of fear,
We'd rather read Hamlet, Caesar, Lear,
By the river of lead where today we stand,
Or carry Juliet, sweet as a kiss,
To her grave, with songs and torches to lead,
Or tremble in darkness as in an abyss
With a hired killer Macbeth will need,—

Only . . . not this, not this, not this,
This we don't have the strength to read!

5.

I warn you, that's the way things are:
This is my final lifetime.
Not as a swallow, reed, or star,
Not as a bell to ring or chime,
Not as the water in a spring,
Not as a maple, branch or beam—
I won't alarm those who are living,
I won't appear in anyone's dream,
Unappeased and unforgiving.

1940

IN MEMORY OF MIKHAIL BULGAKOV

This poem comes to you instead of flowers,
Graveyard roses, or incense smoke;
You who even in the final hours
Showed marvelous disdain. You drank wine. You joked
Like no one else. As for the rest—
You suffocated in a walled-off square;
You yourself admitted the terrible guest,
And remained alone with her there.
Now you don't exist: no one says a thing
About your bitter and beautiful life;
Only my flutelike voice will sing
At this, your silent funeral feast.
It's unbelievable, to say the least,
That I, half-mad, mourning the past,
Smouldering on top of the slowest coal,
Having lost everything and forgotten them all,
Am fated to commemorate someone so strong,
Bright and steady to the final breath—
Was it yesterday we spoke? Has it been so long?—
Who hid the shuddering throes of death.

1940

M. A. Bulgakov: 1891–1940, well-known Russian writer.

One travels straight ahead, the other
In great circles likes to go,
Awaiting return to the home of his father,
Awaiting a girl he used to know.
But when I walk, trouble tags behind,
With a kind of desultory purpose,
We speed into nowhere and never-you-mind,
Like trains plunging over the precipice.

1940

THE FIRST LONG-RANGE
ARTILLERY SHELL IN LENINGRAD

A rainbow of people rushing around,
And suddenly everything changed completely,
This wasn't a normal city sound,
It came from unfamiliar country.
True, it resembled, like a brother,
One peal of thunder or another,
But every natural thunder contains
The moisture of clouds, fresh and high,
And the thirst of fields with drought gone dry,
A harbinger of happy rains,
And this was as arid as hell ever got,
And my distracted hearing would not
Believe it, if only because of the wild
Way it started, grew, and caught,
And how indifferently it brought
Death to my child.

1941

And, in books, I always liked
The last page best,
When the heroine and hero are no longer
Of any interest whatsoever, and so many years
Have passed that you don't pity anyone,
And it seems the author himself
Has forgotten the start of his story,
And even "eternity's turned gray,"
As it says in a wonderful book,
But at this instant, right now,
Everything will end, the author will again
Be irrevocably alone, but he still
Tries to be witty,
Or catty—forgive him, oh Lord!
As he fits a splendid ending,
This one, for example:
. . . And only in two houses
In that town (name blotted out)
There remained a profile (traced by someone
On the snowy whitewash of one wall),
Not a woman's nor a man's, but full of mystery.
And it's said that when the rays of the moon,
Green, low, middle-Asiatic,
Strike these walls at midnight,
Particularly if it's New Year's Eve,
A gentle sound is heard—
Some think it's only crying,
Others make out words in it,
But with this wonder everyone's grown slightly bored,
Tourists are few, the locals are used to it,
And I've heard it said that in one of these houses
They've taken a carpet and covered up the damned
    profile.

1943

63

HOUSEWARMING

to E. S. Bulgakov

1. THE HOSTESS

A sorceress used to live in this place,
Lived in this room before me, I mean:
And still her shadow can be seen
When the new moon shows its face.
Even now her shadow's standing
This side of the doorway,
She looks at me in a certain way,
Both diffident and demanding.
I'm not myself the sort, by and large,
Who falls under another's sway,
I myself . . . But I don't betray
My secrets gratis, free of charge.

1943

2. THE GUESTS

            "You're drunk, my son,
And, besides, it's time to go nach haus . . ."
An aged Don Juan
And a young-again Faust
Have collided by my door, anyway—
From their taverns and rendezvous!
Or was it just the black wind that continues
To make all the branches sway,

E. S. Bulgakov: 1891–1940, widow of the writer.

The green magic of rays,
As if steeped in venom, and even so—
They resemble in repulsive ways
Two people I know.

1943–1944

3. THE BETRAYAL

It wasn't because the mirror shattered,
Or because, in the chimney, the wind howled and leapt,
It wasn't because into my scattered
Thoughts of you something strange had crept,
Those things were chance and nothing more—
They're not the reason I met him at the door.

1943–1944

4. THE TRYST

As if he were in the merry refrain
Of some terrible nursery rhyme,
He walks up the rickety stairs again,
Having conquered separation this time.
Not I to him, but he to me—
Doves in the window, a yard the vines drape,
You are even wearing a cape
As I told you to do, no less.
Not he to me, but I to him, yes—
       in darkness,
              in darkness,
                     in darkness.

1943

THE THREE AUTUMNS

I don't understand summer smiles at all,
And winter holds no charm for me,
Yet as for autumn, almost without fail
I've noticed every year has three.

And the first one is holiday disorder
Spiteful of yesterday's summer fling.
The leaves fly like shreds of notebooks and the odor
Of haze is incense-sweet. Everything
Is moist, many-colored, shining.

The birches are the first to join the dance since they're
Draped in see-through lace and since
They've already shaken off every transient tear
Onto the neighbor over the fence.

Here's what happens when you use a story to
     break the silence:
A second goes by, a minute, and then
Comes the second autumn as dispassionate
     as conscience,
As somber as an air raid siren.

Everyone immediately appears pale and old.
Summer closeness doesn't exist.
And far away trumpets are parading their gold
—Music floats through the fragrant mist.

And in the waves of frankincense, cold and gray,
Is locked the high unflooded land.
But the wind stormed, things opened up,
     and right away
Everyone understood: that's the end of the play.
And this isn't an autumn but death
     showing its hand.

1943

THE BREAKUP

1.

Not weeks, not months—it took us years
To part. And now at last we feel,
Having a gray wreath over our ears,
The breeze of freedom, cool and real.

No more being betrayed and betraying,
And you don't have to listen all night
To the evidence I've been busy arraying
Which proves me incomparably right.

1942

2.

In the breaking-up days, as must always happen,
The ghost of the first days knocked at our door,
And the silvery willow rushed right in,
Gray, glorious branches trailing the floor.

Frenzied, proud, bitter, we stood still
While a blissful bird sang to us from above,
We stood looking down as he sang his fill
About the way we defined our love.

1944

This craft of ours, sacred and bright,
Has lasted too many years to tell . . .
The world is lit by it without light,
But, still, a poet has yet to dwell
On the thought that there's no wisdom or hell,
No age and, perhaps, no death as well.

1944

When the moon is lying on the window sill
Like a slice of casaba, when it's stuffy and
The door's been shut, when houses stand
Transfixed by the blue glycenia's spell,
And there's cold water in a clay cup,
A snowy towel, a candle—Everything
Is as if for a mass. But silence is continuing
To thunder, and something rises up,
Billows out from the fearful dark where it stayed,
From Rembrandtian corners takes shape, unbidden,
Then subsides, sinks back, and again is hidden.
But I'm never going to be afraid . . .
Solitude's trapped me. The landlady's cat, quite
Black, stares like the eye of endless
Years. My mirror-twin is friendless.
I'll sleep soundly. Good night, night!

1944

The souls of all my loved ones are on high stars.
It's good there's no one left to lose,
And I can cry. The air in this town of the tsars
Was made to repeat songs, no matter whose.

A willow among the September brushes
Touches the water, bright and clear.
Risen from the past, my shadow rushes
In silence to meet me here.

So many lyres hang on this tree,
But it seems there's room for mine among these.
And this rain, sparse and sunny,
Is my good tidings and my ease.

1944

CINQUE

It's true I always hated it
When people pitied me.
But you felt pity, stated it—
The sun is new in my body.
That's why dawn is everywhere.
I can do miracles here and there,
That's why!

1945–1946

INSCRIPTION ON A PORTRAIT

Ethereal offspring of the moon's romance,
Marmorial in twilight hedgerows,
Fateful whirler in an old folk dance,
Fairest of all cameos.
People die because such girls are fate,
For such, men were sent by Genghis Khan,
And it was such that on a bloody plate
Carried the head of John.

1946

WILD ROSES ARE BLOOMING
(FROM A BURNED NOTEBOOK)

And thou art distant in humanity . . .

Keats

No normal greeting on a holiday,
But this wind comes, rough and dry, to bring you
A rich aroma of decay,
The taste of smoke and some verses too,
A few poems written in my hand.

4.   FIRST LITTLE SONG

Triumphs, vacant and shuttered,
The mysterious nontryst,
Speeches never uttered,
Words that don't exist.
Looks that do not see
Don't know where to go,
And only tears are happy
That they at length may flow.
The clawing wild roses, alas!
Go with this, hand in glove,
And it will come to pass
They'll call this undying love.

6. THE DREAM

Is it sweet to have unearthly dreams?

A. Blok

Was mine a prophetic dream or wasn't it?
Among the heavenly stars, Mars grew bright:
And shone with an ominous light, sparkling, scarlet.
I dreamed of your arrival late that night.

You appeared in everything—the Bach chaconne,
And in the roses that bloomed but had no worth,
In the church bells ringing there for no one,
And in the yielding blackness of plowed earth,

And in the fall which approached as if for a kiss,
And suddenly changed its mind and ran away.
Oh, August, how could you bring me news like this
On the anniversary of that awful day?

The kingly gift who knows how one repays?
With whom should I exchange a victor's look?
And so I work as carefully as always,
Writing verses in a burned notebook.

8.

You invented me. No such person exists, that's for sure,
There's no such creature anywhere in sight.
No poet can quench my thirst, no physician has a cure,
The shadow of your ghost haunts me day and night.
We met in an unbelievable year,
The energies of the world were worn through,

The world was in mourning, everything sagged with
    fear,
And only the graves were new.
In the absence of light, how black the Neva grew,
The deaf night surrounded us like a wall . . .
That's exactly when I called out to you!
What I was doing—I didn't yet understand at all.
And, as if led by a star you came to me,
As if walking on a carpet the tragic autumn had grown,
Into that house ravaged for the rest of eternity,
From whence a flock of burned verses has flown.

9.   IN THE BROKEN MIRROR

Incorrigible words I listened to
That night of stars too bright for names,
And my head was spinning as if it knew
It hung above an abyss of flames
Close by, destruction set up a howl
And the black orchard flew off like an owl
And, mortally weakened, on its rocky shelf
The town was then older than Troy itself.
That hour flared unbearably bright.
It rang, it seemed, till it made tears come.
You didn't give me the gift you brought,
The gift you'd carried a long way home.
On that fiery evening you thought it vain,
You thought such amusements had to wait.
And so it became a honeyed bane
In my mysterious fate.
It made straight the way for the troubles I face,
Let's not remember it any more!
The meeting that somehow did not take place
Still sobs outside the door.

1956

MUSIC

for D.D.S.

A flame burns within her, miraculously,
While you look, her edges crystallize.
She alone will draw near and speak to me
When others are afraid to meet my eyes.
She was with me even in my grave
When the last of my friends turned away,
And she sang like the first storm heaven gave,
Or as if flowers were having their say.

1958

Dimitri D. Shostakovitch: 1906–1975, great Russian composer.

SEASIDE SONNET

Everything here will outlive me—Everything,
Even those ramshackly birdhouses there
And all this air, this springtime air,
That has made the oceanic crossing.

And the voice of eternity is calling
Otherworldly, irresistible,
And over the cherry tree, blooming, full,
The moon's brilliant light is falling.

And the road running easy and white,
In emerald thickets is lost to sight,
I don't know where it will end . . .

It's lighter among the trees,
It's all like the paths one sees
By the Tsarskoselsky pond.

1958

THE SECRETS OF THE CRAFT

3. MUSE

A burden I can't lighten or lose,
And yet most people call her "Muse"—
They say: "In meadows you receive her . . ."
"Ravings," they say, "Divine as they come . . ."
She'll toss you about more roughly than fever,
And then for more than a year keep mum.

1959

6. THE LAST POEM

One, like thunder someone's scared a bit
With a breath of life, rushes to where I sit,
Laughs and quivers, just outside my throat,
Then spins and applauds as if striking the proper note.

Another, born in midnight's still despair,
Likes sneaking up on me from who knows where,
Looks at me out of an empty mirror,
Murmuring sternly as soon as it comes clearer.

And some are like this: in the middle of the day,
Almost as if they don't see me, they come my way,
They stream over the white paper I've left,
They flow like a pure spring in a rocky cleft.

Or else: something secret wanders around—
It isn't a sound or a color, not color, not sound,
It crystallizes like a prism, it changes, twists,
But it won't surrender as long as it exists.

But this! It drank all the blood which it had wrung
From me, nasty as love when I was young,
It looked as though it would say a word and then
It turned back into wordlessness again.

And I have never known a crueler trouble,
It left, and yet its tracks still stretch out, double,
To the endless end of denying,
While I, without it, am dying.

1959

7.   EPIGRAM

Could Beatrice, like Dante, describe those final places,
Or Laura celebrate the fire of love's embraces?
I taught women how to speak in many cases,
But now—oh God—how to make them shut their faces!

1960

9.

To Osip Mandelstam

How spicy is the scent carnations give,
The carnations I dreamed of at one time there;
There, where the circling Eurydices live,
Where Europa rides the bull, and where
Our shadows fleet across the river;
They cross the Neva, your reality,
Where city steps make the Neva shiver,—
This is your passport to immortality.

1940–1960

Osip Mandelstam: see note, page 53.

Don't threaten me with a terrible fate
And huge boredom, that northern creation.
Today's a day to celebrate,
A holiday named separation.
We didn't wait up for the dawn—okay.
We didn't watch the moon careen,
But I'll endow you with gifts today
Such as the world has never seen:
My image in the water at the time of night
Rivers can't sleep even if they try,
A look that didn't help a bright
Falling star return to the sky,
The echo of a voice now exhausted, unclear,
But then as fresh as summer grows,—
So you'll be able to attend without fear
The gossip of Moscovian crows,
So a damp fall day will cast a spell
More sweet than the bliss any May can know . . .
Do remember me, my angel,
At least until it starts to snow.

1959

TO THE MEMORY OF A POET

Like a bird, echo will answer me.

B.P. (Boris Pasternak)

1.

That singular voice has stopped: silence is complete,
And the one who spoke with forests has left us behind.
He turned himself into a life-giving stalk of wheat
Or the fine rain his songs can call to mind.
And all the flowers that hold this world in debt
Have come into bloom, come forward to meet this
   death.
But everything stood still on the planet
Which bears the unassuming name . . . the Earth.

2.

Like the daughter of Oedipus the blind,
Toward death the Muse was leading the seer.
And one linden tree, out of its mind,
Was blooming that mournful May, near
The window where he told me one time
That before him rose a golden hill,
With a winged road that he would climb,
Protected by the highest will.

1960

Boris Pasternak: 1890–1960, renowned Russian poet and novelist.

REQUIEM

No, it wasn't under a foreign heaven,
It wasn't under the wing of a foreign power,—
I was there among my countrymen,
I was where my people, unfortunately, were.

1961

INSTEAD OF A PREFACE

In the awful years of Yezhovian horror, I spent seventeen months standing in line in front of various prisons in Leningrad. One day someone "recognized" me. Then a woman with blue lips, who was standing behind me, and who, of course, had never heard my name, came out of the stupor which typified all of us, and whispered into my ear (everyone there spoke only in whispers):

—Can you describe this?

And I said:

—I can.

Then something like a fleeting smile passed over what once had been her face.

April 1, 1957
Leningrad

N. I. Yezhov: head of the NKVD, the Soviet Secret Police from 1936 to 1938, was noted for his ferocity. He presided over the great purges, and the period of 1936–1938 is therefore known as "Yezhovshchina."

DEDICATION

Faced with this grief, mountains sink down,
The great river has to languish,
But the hasps of the prison are made of iron,
And behind them the "concentration den"
And deadly anguish.
Cool winds are stroking someone's hair,
And the sun is shining on someone's head—
We don't know, we're the same everywhere,
The gnashing of keys is all we hear
And the soldiers' booted tread.
We get up as if there were priests to assist,
We cross the rebrutalized city squares,
More breathless than the dead, we come to the tryst,
The sun is lower and the Neva's all mist,
And far off, the song of hoping flares.
Sentence . . . And at once the tears will start,
How different from the others one's already grown,
It's as if they took the life out of the heart,
Like being thrown backwards on a jolting cart,
. . . She's coming . . . Staggering . . . Alone . . .
Where now are all the chance-met people,
Friends during those two years in hell?
Of which Siberian storms are they full?
What phantoms do they see in the lunar circle?
It's to them I am sending this farewell.

1940

INTRODUCTION

This happened when only the dead wore smiles—
They rejoiced at being safe from harm.
And Leningrad dangled from its jails

83

Like some unnecessary arm.
And when the hosts of those convicted,
Marched by—mad, tormented throngs,
And train whistles were restricted
To singing separation songs.
The stars of death stood overhead,
And guiltless Russia, that pariah,
Writhed under boots, all blood-bespattered,
And the wheels of many a black maria.

1935

3.

No, this isn't me, someone else suffers,
I couldn't stand it. All that's happened
They should wrap up in black covers,
The streetlights should be taken away . . .
                    Night.

1939

4.

They should have shown you, girl of the clever hello
And the scoffing darling of many a friend,
The happy sinner from Tsarskoe Selo,
What would happen to your life before the end—
Carrying bundles, the three-hundredth soul
Waiting at the Cross Prison door,
And your warm tear would burn a hole
In the new year's icy floor.
The prison poplar continues to bend,
There's not a sound to be heard—but how many
Innocent lives are coming to an end . . .

1939

5.

For months I've filled the air with pleas,
Trying to call you back.
I've thrown myself at the hangman's knees,
You are my son and my rack.
From now on, categories spill,
And I no longer have any solution—
Who's a beast, who's human still,
How long I must wait for the execution.
Besides dusty flowers, there is also
The ringing of censers, and tracks that go
From somewhere into nowhere fast.
And straight ahead, there's this to see:
A gigantic star, threatening me
With death when a day or two have passed.

1939

Epilogue

I

I've seen how a face can fall like a leaf,
How, from under the lids, terror peeks,
I've seen how suffering and grief
Etches hieroglyphs on cheeks,
How ash-blonde hair, from roots to tips,
Turns black and silver overnight.
How smiles wither on submissive lips,
And in a half-smile quivers fright.
Not only for myself do I pray,
But for those who stood in front and behind me,
In the bitter cold, on a hot July day
Under the red wall that stared blindly.

II

Again the memorial hour's drawing near.
You are the one I see and feel and hear:

Who was barely able to come to the window and stand,
The one who does not tread her native land.

Who looked at me and tossed her beautiful head,
And "Coming here is coming home," she said.

I'd like to call each one by name, in turn,
But someone took my list away to burn.

For them I've woven a wide shroud today
Of insufficient words I heard them say.

I've thought about them everywhere I've been,
I won't forget them in the new misfortune.

Someone might close my lips, I have no doubt,
Through which a hundred million people shout,

Let them remember me the selfsame way,
On the eve of my memorial day.

And if it ever be this land's intent
To honor me with any monument,

I give permission to that future nation,
With one condition, for the celebration:

Don't put it in my birthplace, ocean-battered,
My last connection with the sea's been shattered,

Nor in the Czar's park by the hallowed tree,*
Where an inconsolable spirit looks for me,

But here where for three hundred hours I had to wait,
And still they didn't open that certain gate.

Because even in blissful death I'd be afraid
To forget the clatter black marias made,

To forget the way the hated door slammed shut
And an old lady wailed like a wounded creature, but

Let from the lids of bronze, unmoving eyes
Snow melt and stream like the tears each human cries,

And let in the distance the prison pigeons coo,
While along the Neva, ships pass quietly through.

1940

*This tree or stump in Tsarskoe Selo often figures in Akhmatova's poetry. It connects her with Pushkin, symbolizes her ties to Russian poetic tradition, etc.

QUATRAIN SEQUENCE (SELECTIONS)

Marble crumbles, steel rots like a leaf,
Gold rusts. Everything's ready to die.
The most durable things on earth are grief
And a single word, majestically high.

1945

TO MY POEMS

You led me into the trackless woods,
My falling stars, my dark endeavor.
You were bitterness, lies, a bill of goods.
You weren't a consolation—ever.

1961

Fiery eyes, believe me,
You smile like Venus's son . . .
I beg you, don't deceive me,
April, day number one!

1963

MY NAME

From out of nowhere it came,
Murky, a Tartar claim.
It sticks a pin in my bubble,
The name for this name is trouble.

1962

Swimming in a golden haze,
Swanlike, fame was there.
As for you, love, you were always—
Always my despair.

1962

LISTENING TO SINGING

A woman's voice, like the wind, rushes—
Nocturnal it seems, moist and black,
And as it flies, whatever it brushes
Changes and will not change back.
Its diamond-shine comes to bathe and bless,
Things are draped in a silver light,
It rustles its suggestive dress,
Woven of fantasy, silken and bright.
And the power that propels the enchanted
Voice displays such hidden might,
It's as if the grave were not ahead,
But mysterious stairs beginning their flight.

1961

THE LAST ROSE

You will write about us on a slant

J. Brodsky

With Morozova I should bow and obey,
I should rise with the smoke from Dido's pyre,
I should dance with Salome,
And thus be again with Joan in the fire.

Oh Lord! You see how tired one grows
Of resurrection, and dying, and living,
Take it all except this crimson rose—
Let me feel the freshness of the gift it's giving.

1962

F. P. Morozova: 1632–1675, called Feodora after she became a nun, a saint in the Old Believers' church. She was a follower of Avvakum, and died in prison as a martyr.

MIDNIGHT VERSES

Seven Poems

A mirror dreams only of another mirror,
Silence watches over silence . . .

"Reshka"

Instead of a Dedication

I hide in the forest and wander the ocean too,
I'm in enamel, but can be seen without it.
I can probably stand being apart from you,
But as for our meeting, I rather doubt it.

1. Pre-Spring Elegy

. . . toi qui m'a consolée
Gerard de Nerval

The snowstorm's abated within the stand of pine,
Silence sang to us as Ophelia might,
Drunk as she was even without wine,
Silence herself sang to us there all night.
And he whom I saw only as I saw my breath
Was betrothed to that silent maid.
He took his leave, then generously stayed.
He stayed with me even unto death.

"Reshka": A poem by Akhmatova written in 1941. This quote is from stanza 8, the last two lines. *Reshka* is "tails" in Russian coin-tossing.

2. THE FIRST WARNING

When it comes down to it, what do we care
That everything finally turns into dust,
Over how many abysses I sang in despair,
Or in how many mirrors I lived as I must?
So I'm not a dream, not a comfort, not good,
And least of all am I a blessing,
But you'll recall more often than you should—
I'm not sure, of course, I'm only guessing—
The rumble of lines which are quieting down,
And the eye concealing on its floor
That rusted little thorny crown
In its uneasy silence, and more.

3. THROUGH THE LOOKING-GLASS

O quae beatam, Diva, tenes Cyprum et Memphin . . .*
                                                    Horace

The cute girl is very young but she
Is from a different century than ours,
The two of us can never be
Alone, the third will never go.
I generously share with her my flowers,
You bring a chair so she can sit in it . . .
What we are doing, we don't ourselves know,
But we're more frightened with each passing minute.
Like people who've just gotten out of jail,
We know something awful, have terrible things to tell
About each other. We're in a circle of hell,
But then, maybe it's not us at all.

   *"O, Goddess, who rules over the happy Cyprus and Memphis
. . ." (Horace, *Odes* 3:26).

4. THIRTEEN LINES

Finally you have uttered the word
Not like those others . . . who kneel on just one knee,
But like one who's escaped from captivity
And who sees birches standing in their hallowed shade
Through a rainbow involuntary tears have made.
And silence began to sing around you,
The dusk was lit by the pure sun and warmed,
And the world for a moment was transformed
And what wine there was tasted strangely new.
Even I, who was to take a knife
And murder the holy word impenitently,
Fell silent almost reverently
In order to prolong that blessed life.

5. THE CALL

In a sonata as if in a quilt
I will hide you away so you can't crawl out.
Oh! How anxiously you'll call out,
Full of irreparable guilt
For having approached me,
If for a moment only . . .
Your dream is—disappearance,
To a place where death's just a sacrifice to silence.

6. NIGHT VISIT

Everyone left, and no one came back.

You won't wait on a path that's asphalty,
Or in a leaf-covered street.

But in some adagio by Vivaldi
Again we'll meet.
The candles will show a dim yellow flame,
Bewitched by sleep,
But the bow won't ask how it was you came
To my midnight keep.
In lamentation, deadly and calm,
We'll pass an hour or more,
You, of course, will read in my palm
Such wonders as before.
And then that great anxiety
Which is now your doom
Will lead you into the icy sea,
Far from me and my room.

7.   AND THE LAST ONE

Above us was something like a star above the sea,
Searching for the deadly ninth wave with its ray.
You called it a bane and an adversity;
"Joy" was a word you never thought to say.

Like a swallow it circled before us during the day,
Smiles bloomed on its lips. But it knew no pity
At night—it choked us with its icy hand,
Both at once. And you were in a different city.

Ignoring our praises, and having blotted out
All the previous sins and curses,
It leans on the insomniest pillows we've got
And mutters its damnable verses.

1963

Instead of an Afterword

Where they invented dreams and made them flower,
They didn't have enough to go around,
We saw the same one, yes, but it had power
In it, as when spring first hits the ground.

1965

All of Moscow is soaked with verses,
Skewered with meter time after time.
Let wordlessness rule over us,
Let us live apart from rhyme.
Let muteness be the secret badge
Of those with you who seem like me,
And you unite in a secret marriage
With the purest, bitterest silence—She
Who etches granite as water licks,
Who makes the magic circle round,
Who whispers into your ear and predicts
Your death, overcoming the loudest sound.

1963

It's not with a lover's lyre, not at all,
That I go around, attracting a crowd.
It's the rattle with which lepers crawl
That in my hands keeps singing aloud.

1964

Where nothing is needed, I walk like a child,
My shadow serves as the friend I crave.
The wind breezes out of a grove gone wild,
And my foot is on the edge of the grave.

1964

ON THE ROAD

This land isn't native to me and still
It's given me memories time can't erase,
In its sea, water is tenderly chill,
Of salt it bears not a single trace.

The air intoxicates like wine,
Under the sea is sand, chalk-white.
And the rosy body of every pine
Is denuded as sunset beckons night.

And the sunset itself in waves of ether
Is such that I can't say with certainty
Whether day is ending, or the world, or whether
The secret of secrets is again in me.

1964–1965